GUITAR MUSIC OF CUBA

A collection of popular Cuban music edited & arranged by **John Zaradin** for solo guitar

Chester Music Limited
(A division of Music Sales Limited)
8/9 Frith Street, London W1V 5TZ

Introduction

Left hand fingerings...

1 2 3 4 0

1st, 2nd, 3rd and 4th fingers of
the left hand and open string.
When used with chords or clusters of notes
they are reserved for the top and/or
bottom note(s) of those chords or clusters.

Right hand fingerings...

p i m a e

Thumb, 1st, 2nd, 3rd and
4th fingers of the right hand.

↑ Rasgueado, with fingers (as indicated)
striking the chord from the bass strings
to the treble.

↓ Rasgueado striking the chord from
the treble strings to the bass.

Tablature...

Can be read directly or used as a
cross-reference for the left hand fingering
positions marked in the notation.

Fingerboard position markings...

I II III IV V *etc*

Indicate that the first finger of the left
hand moves to and plays at the fret marked.

CI CII CIII CIV CV *etc*

Indicate that the first finger of the left
hand makes a bar and holds all 6 strings at
the fret marked.

½CI ½CII ½CIII ½CIV ½CV *etc*

Indicate that the first finger of the
left hand makes a bar stretching across to
the second, third, fourth or fifth string at
the fret marked.

String markings...

① ② ③ ④ ⑤ ⑥

The 1st, 2nd, 3rd, 4th, 5th and 6th strings
of the guitar.

Harmonics (open)...

◆ **Diamond shaped notehead**
Place a finger of the left hand directly over
the fret indicated on the tablature score.

We have endeavoured to
trace all copyright holders
but will be pleased to
rectify any omissions notified
to us in future reprints.

This book © Copyright
1999 by Chester Music.
Order No. CH61433
ISBN 0-7119-6855-1

Music setting by
Enigma Music Production Services.
Book design by Michael Bell Design.
Cover illustration by Angela Dundee.
Printed in Great Britain by
Printwise (Haverhill) Limited, Suffolk.

Mama Son De La Loma 4
The Breeze And I 9
La Comparsa 14
Malagueña 20
Habanera 28
Lágrimas Negras 32
The Peanut Vendor 34
Solamente Una Vez 38
Frenesí 40
Guajira Margarita 44
Guajira San Juan 48
Cachita 56
Siempre En Mi Corazón 59

Mama Son De La Loma

Miguel Matamoros
Arr. John Zaradin

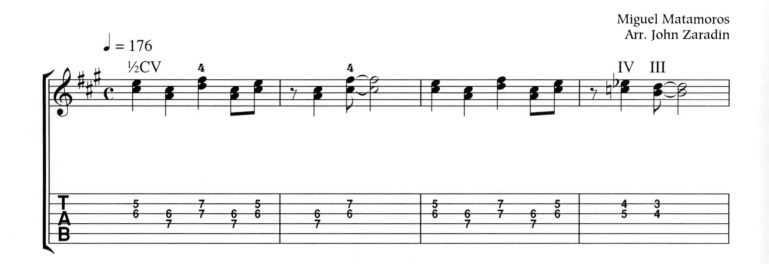

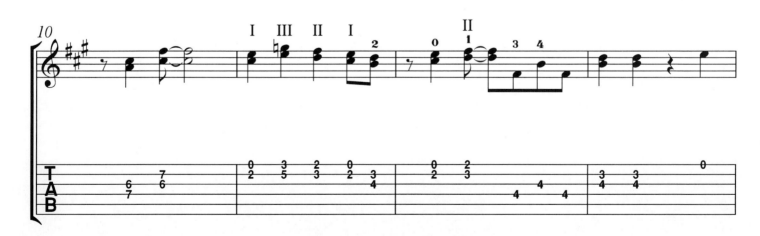

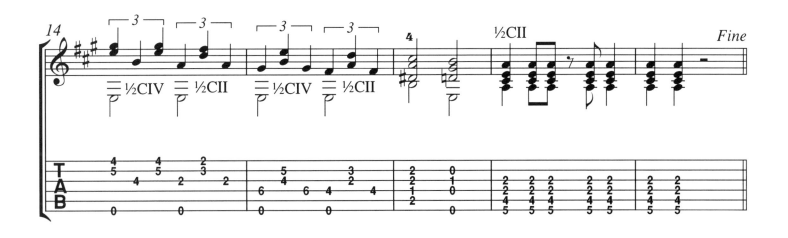

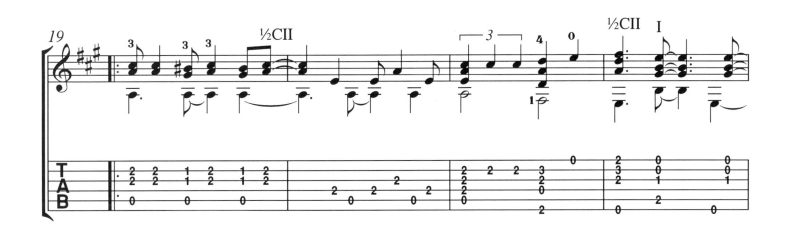

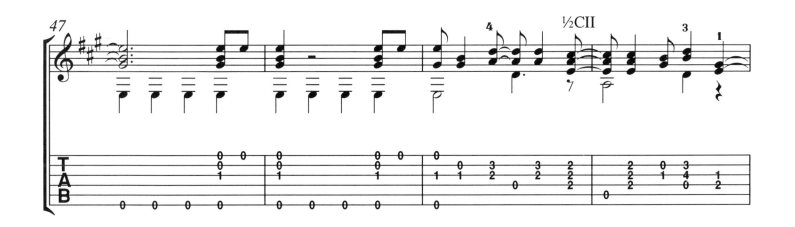

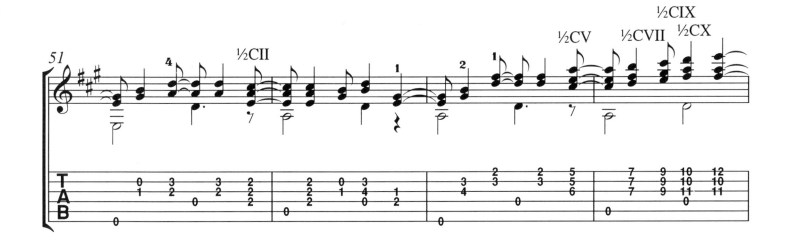

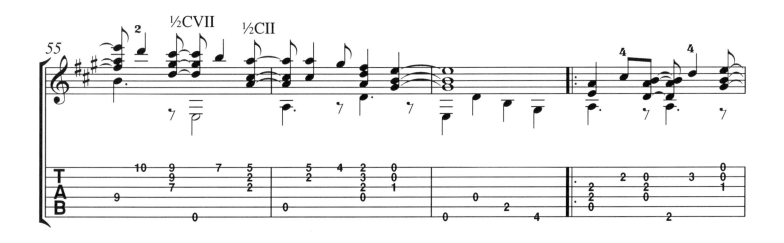

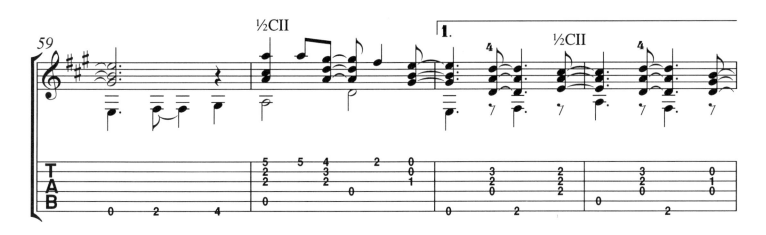

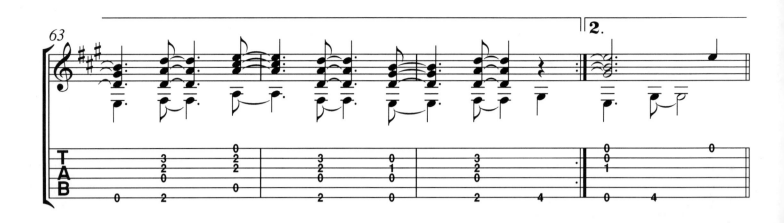

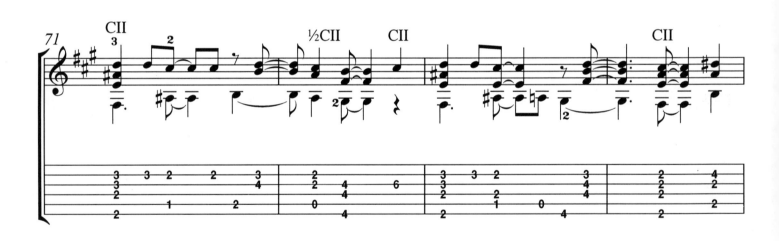

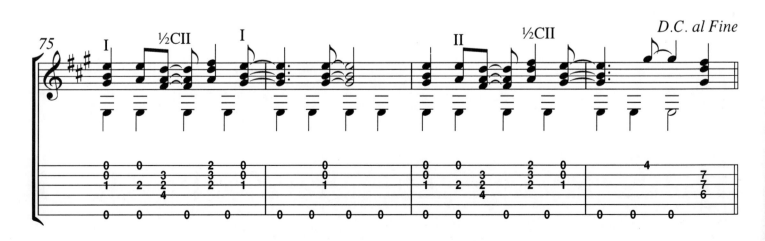

The Breeze And I

Ernesto Lecuona
Arr. John Zaradin

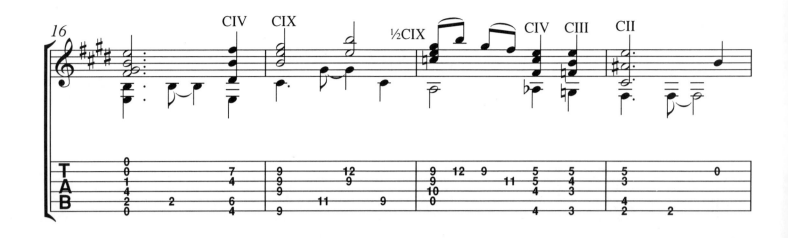

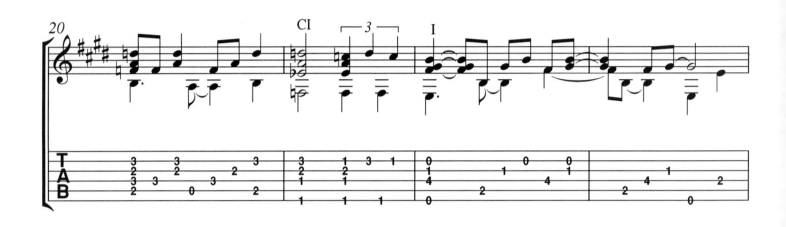

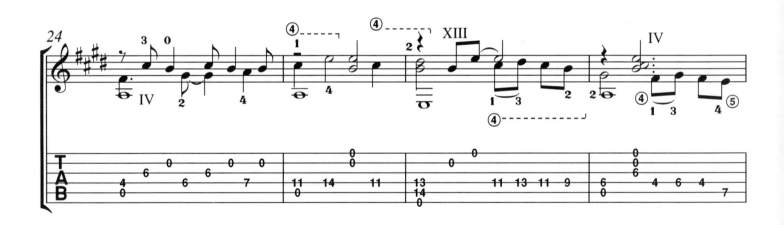

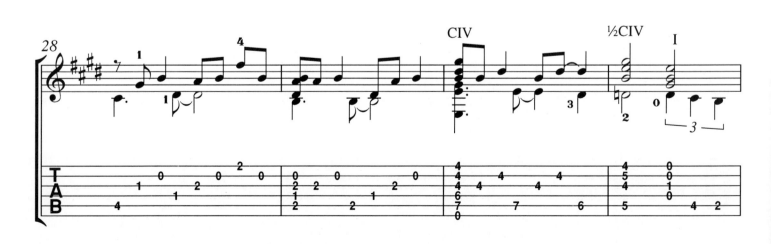

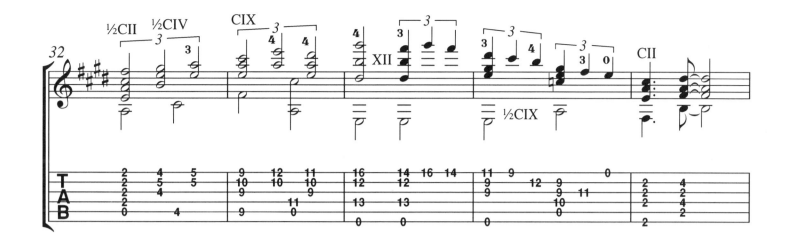

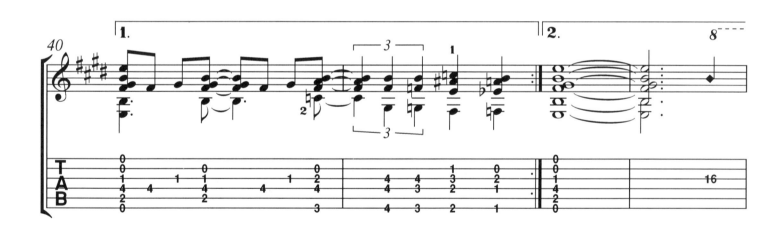

(Tablature fret number indicates Right Hand position placing. See score notes)

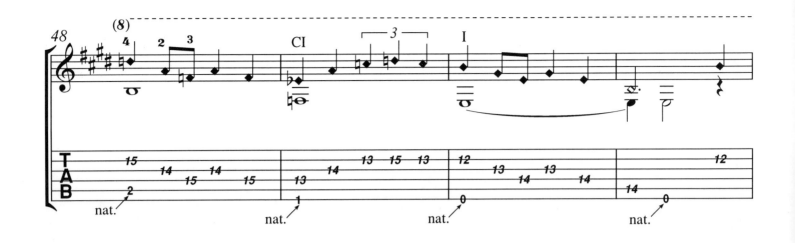

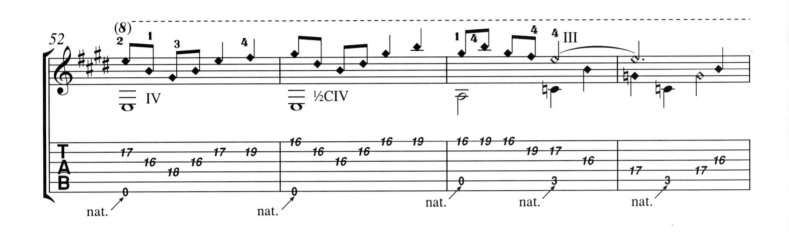

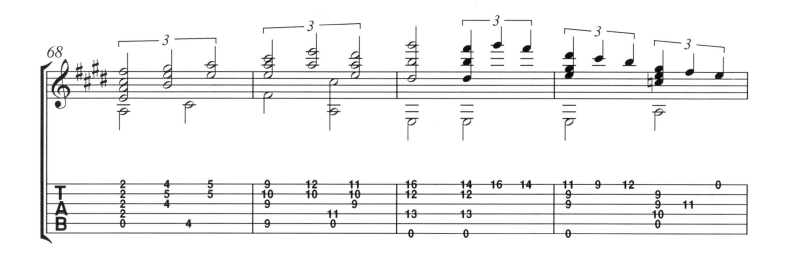

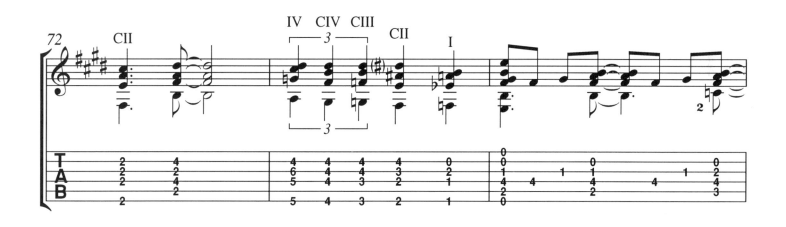

La Comparsa

Ernesto Lecuona
Arr. John Zaradin

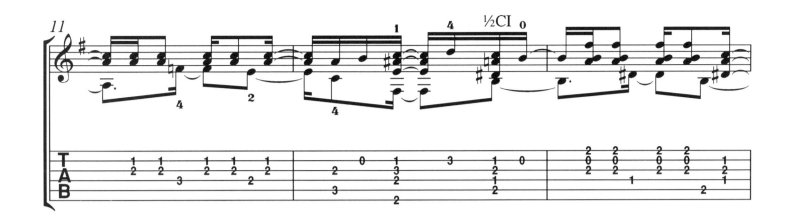

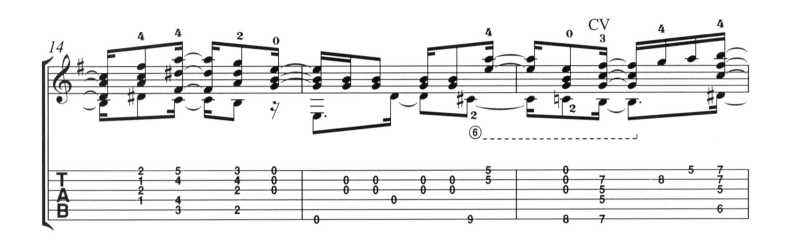

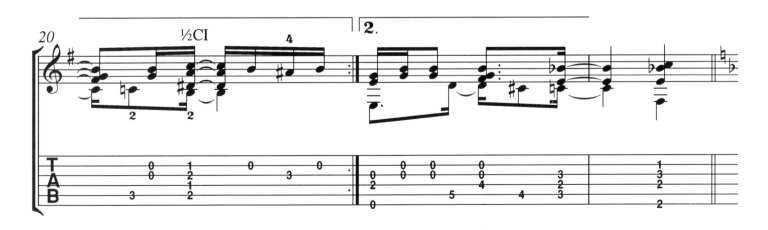

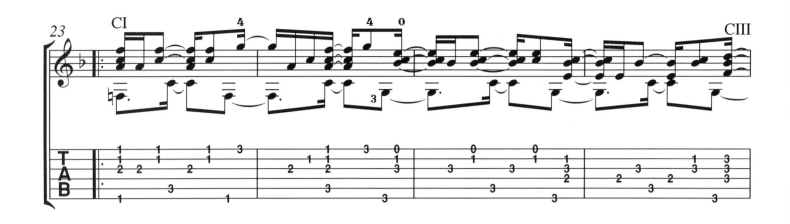

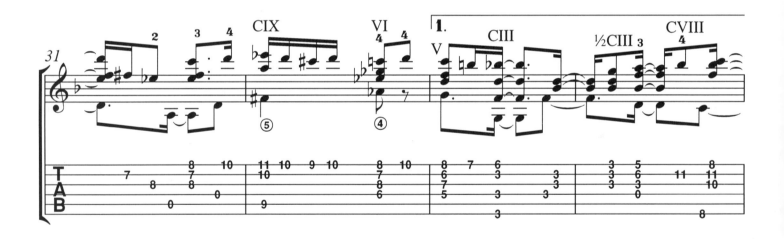

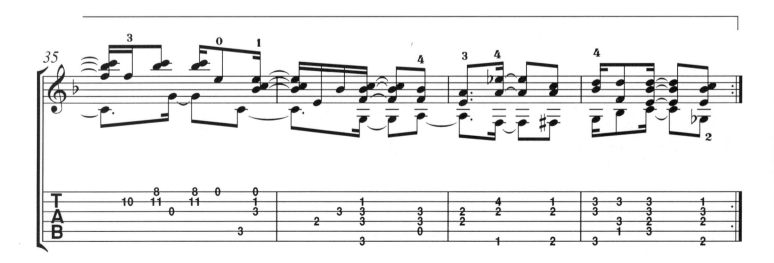

Malagueña

Ernesto Lecuona
Arr. John Zaradin

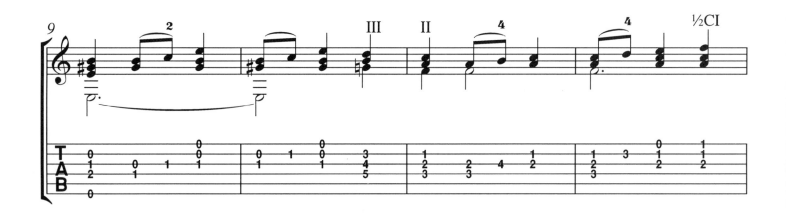

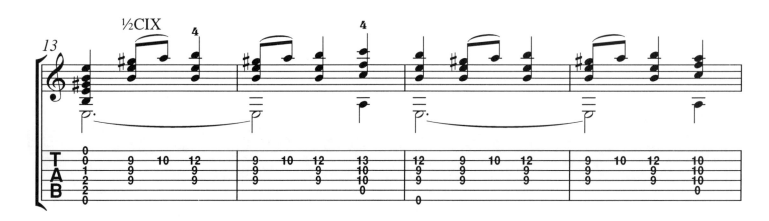

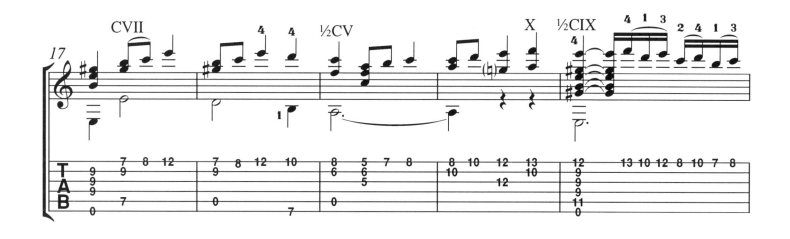

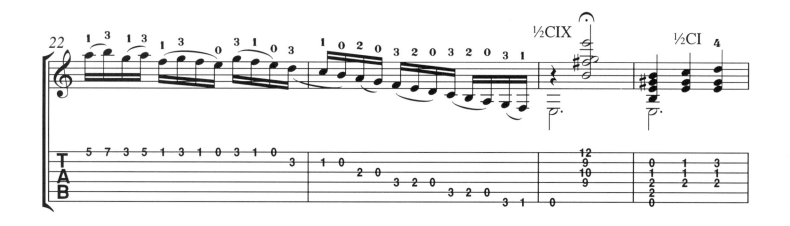

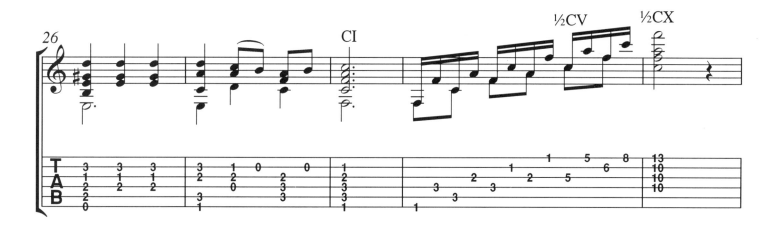

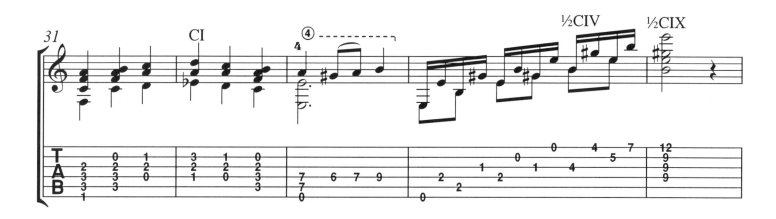

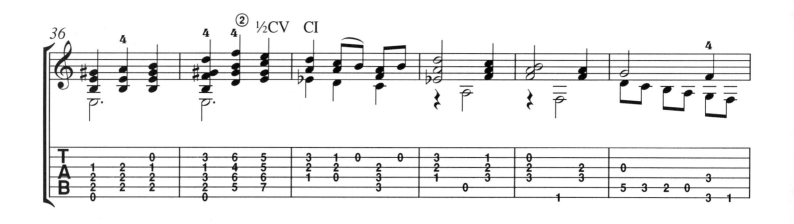

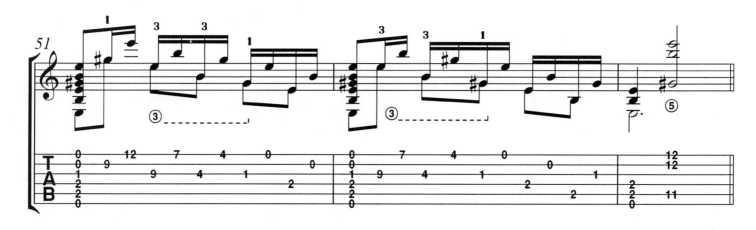

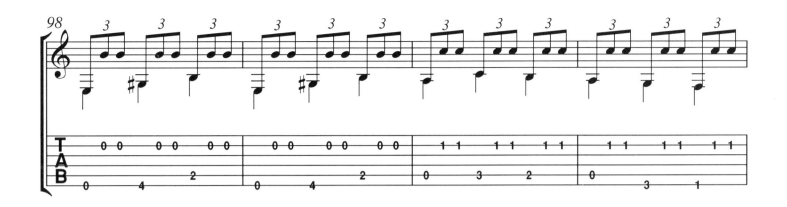

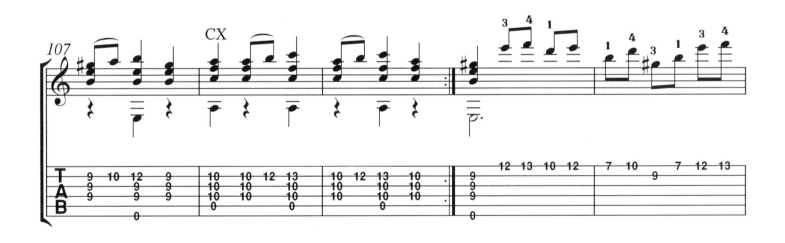

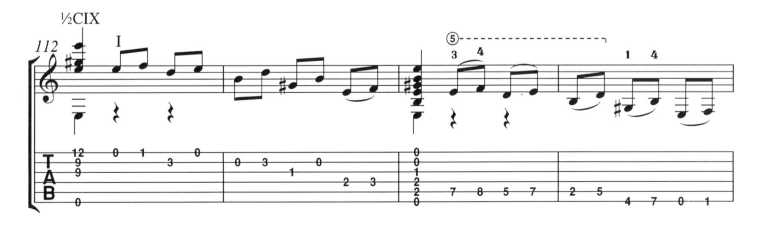

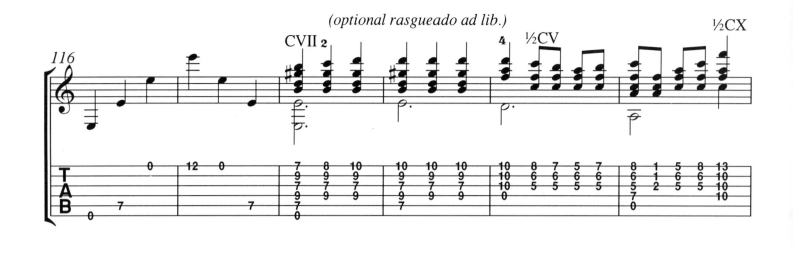

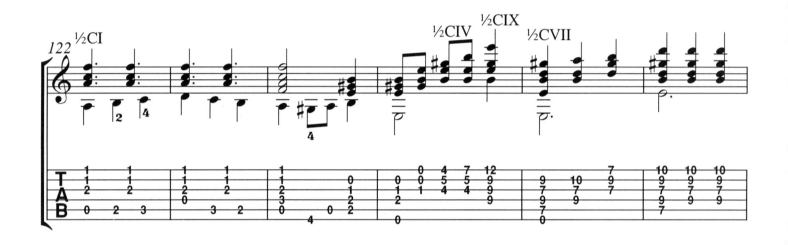

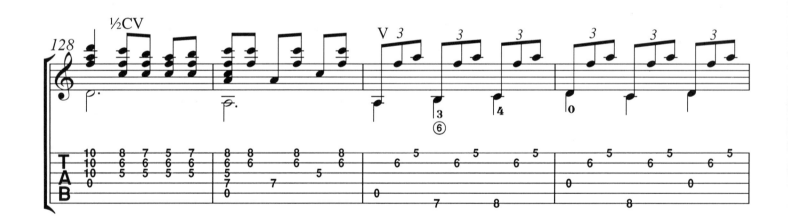

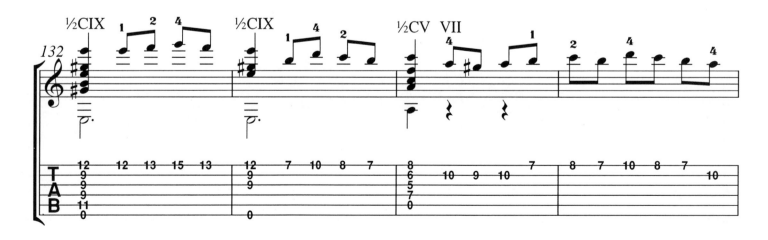

Habanera
from Carmen

Georges Bizet
Arr. John Zaradin

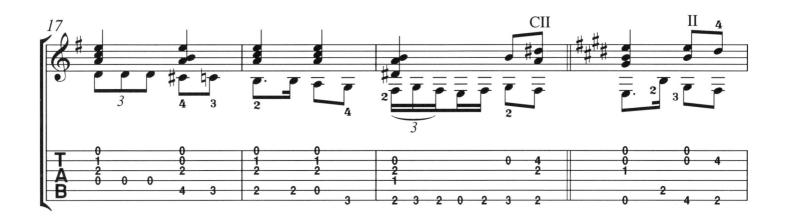

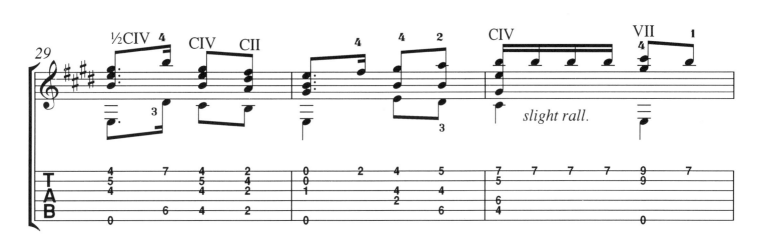

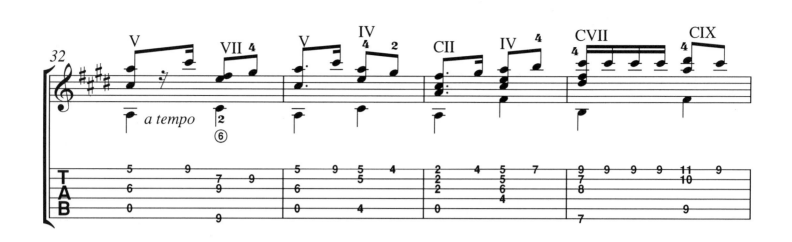

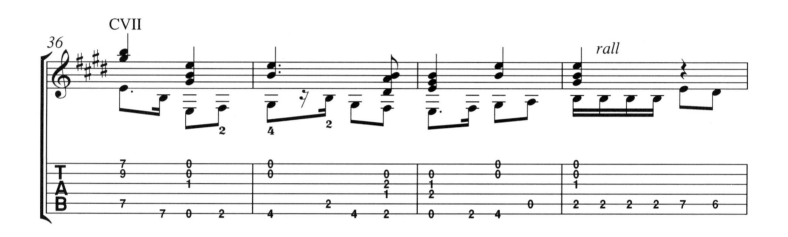

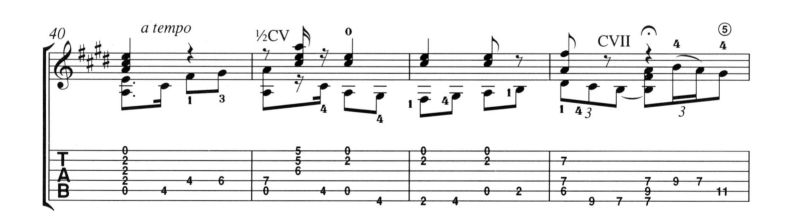

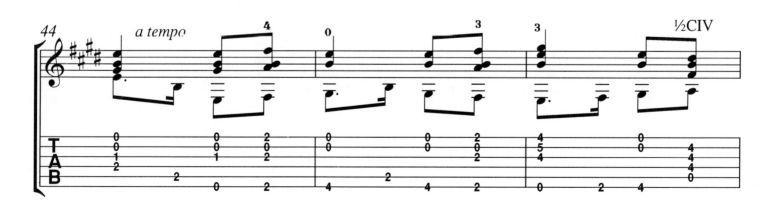

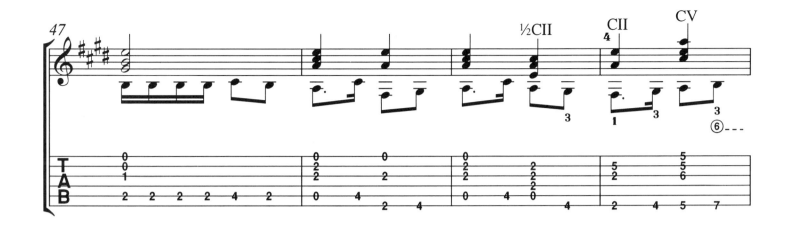

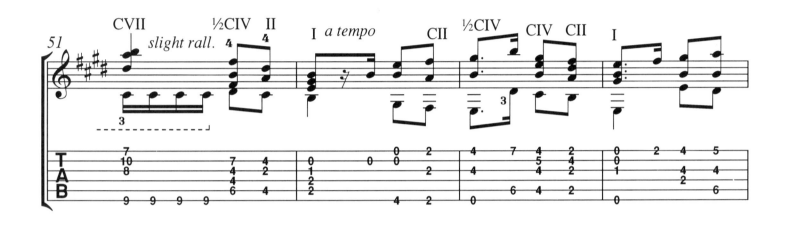

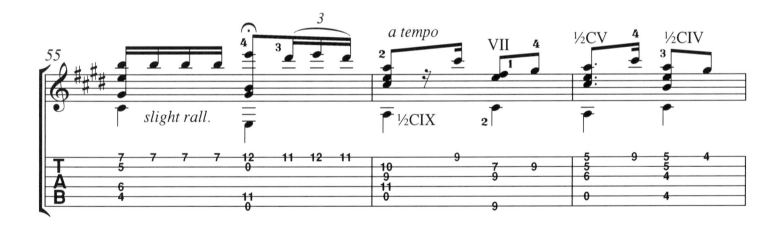

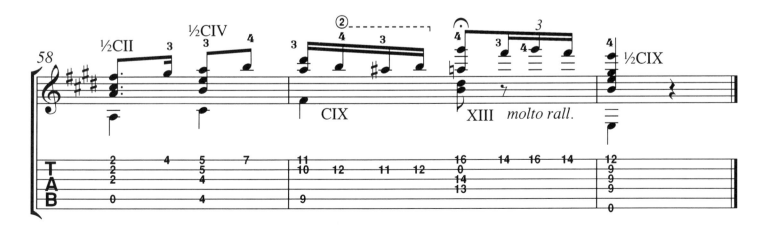

Lágrimas Negras

Miguel Matamoros
Arr. John Zaradin

repeat SON ad lib. & fade

33

The Peanut Vendor
El Manicero

Moises Simons
Arr. John Zaradin

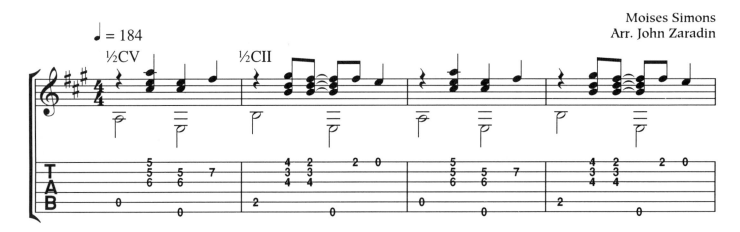

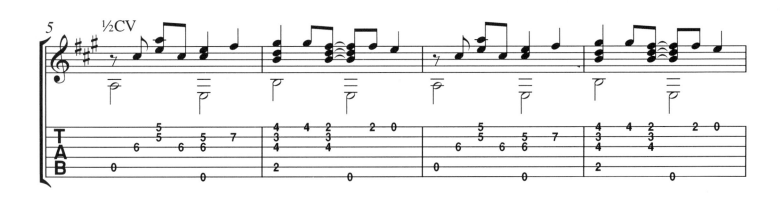

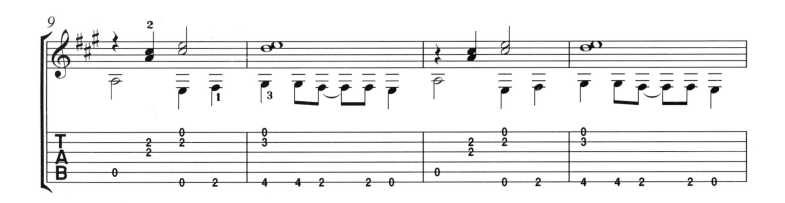

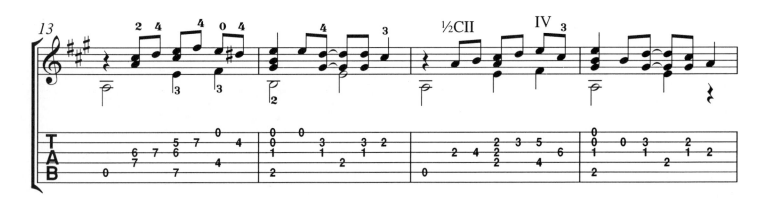

Solamente Una Vez

Bolero

Agustín Lara
Arr. John Zaradin

Frenesí

Alberto Dominguez
Arr. John Zaradin

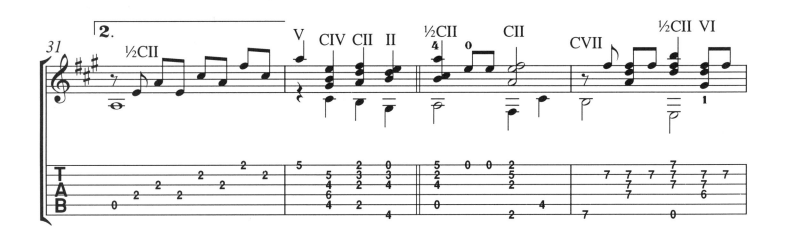

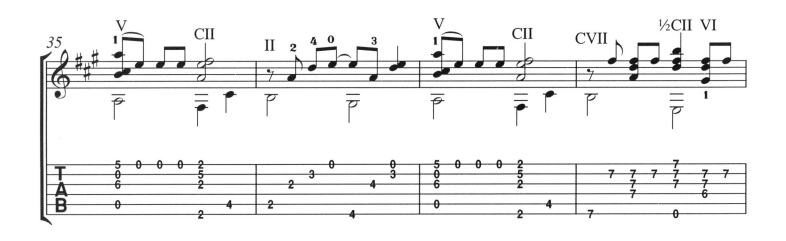

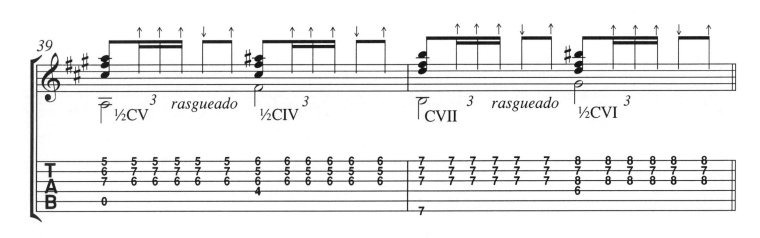

Guajira Margarita

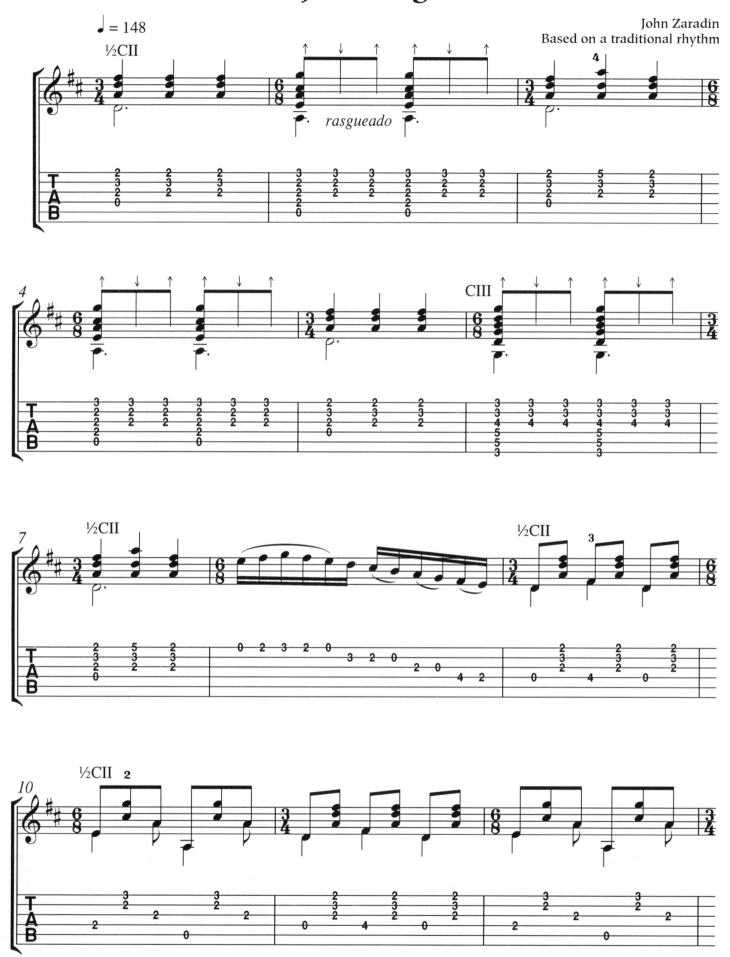

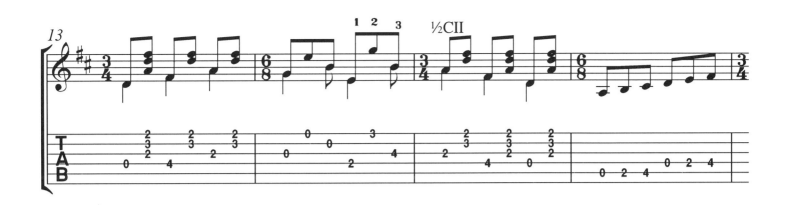

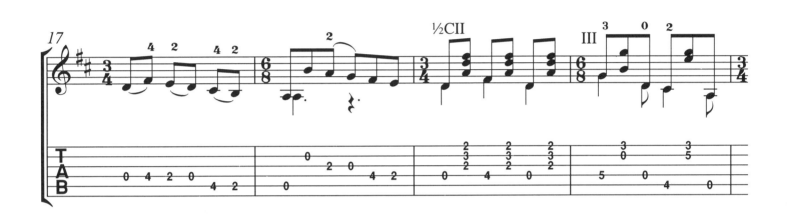

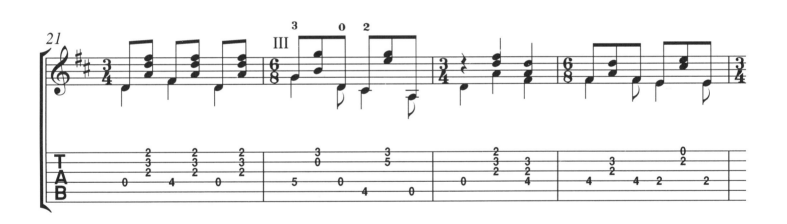

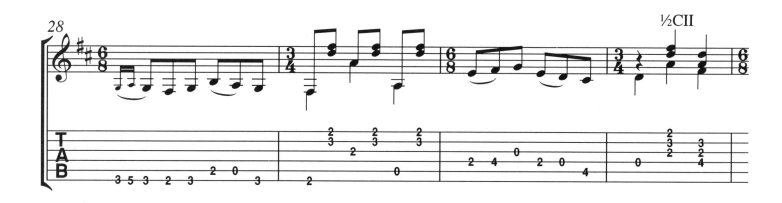

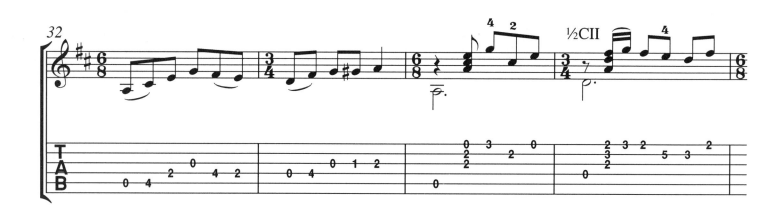

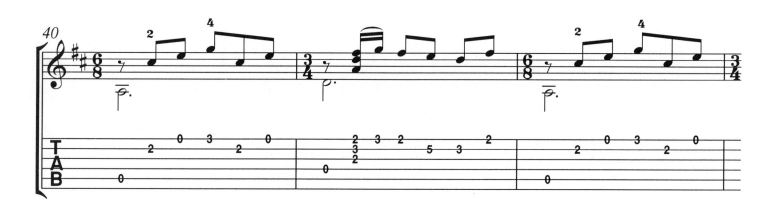

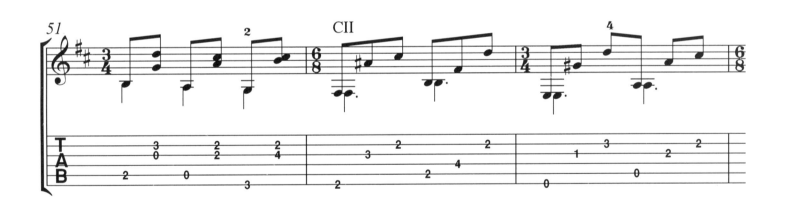

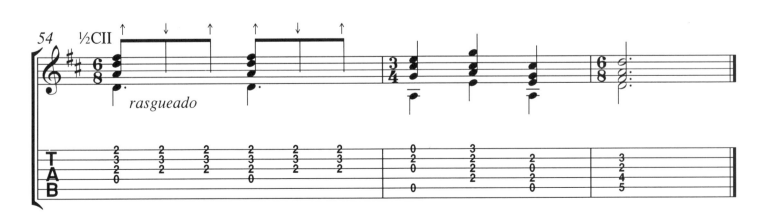

Guajira San Juan

John Zaradin
Based on a traditional rhythm

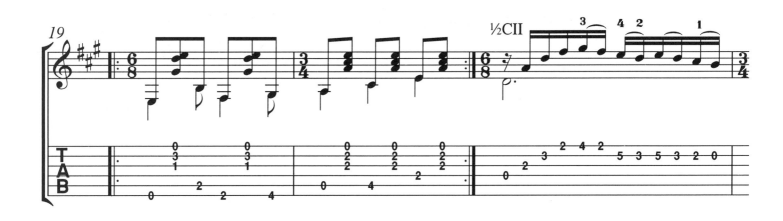

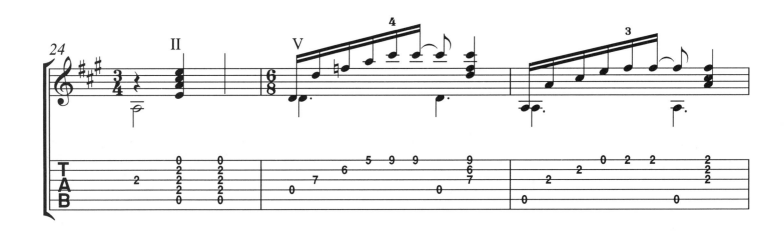

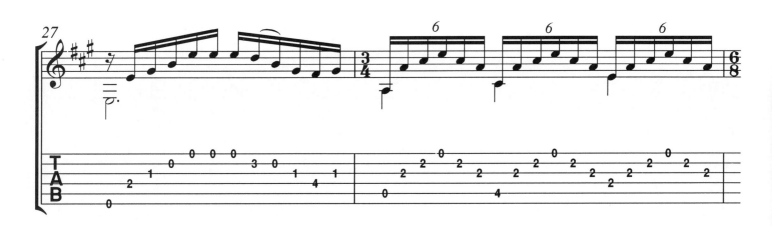

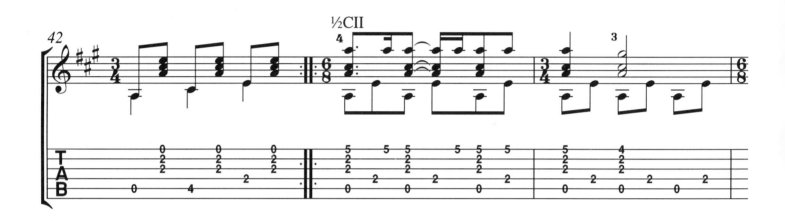

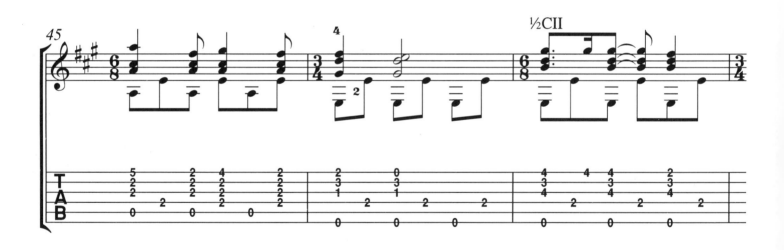

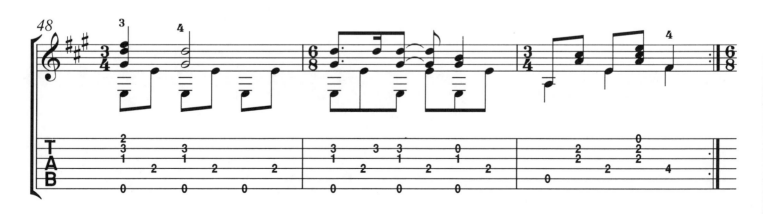

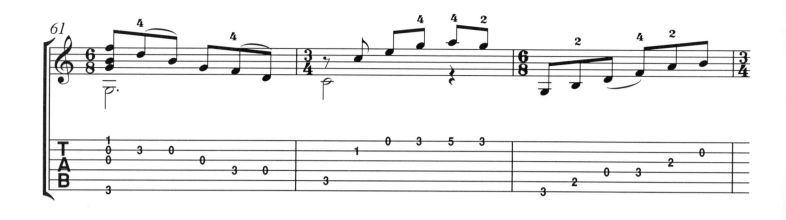

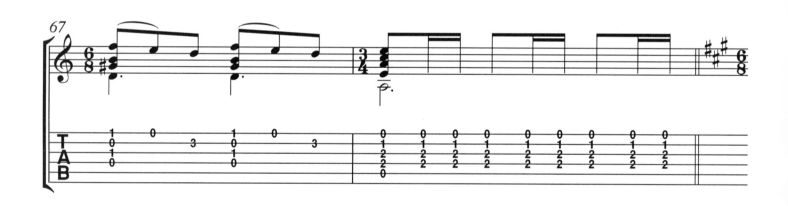

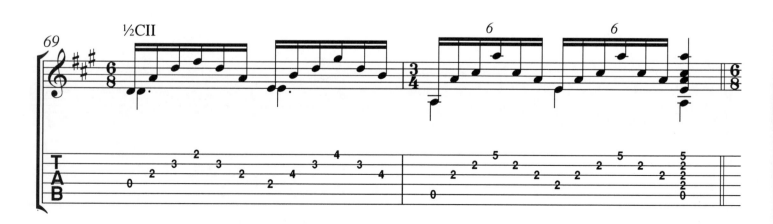

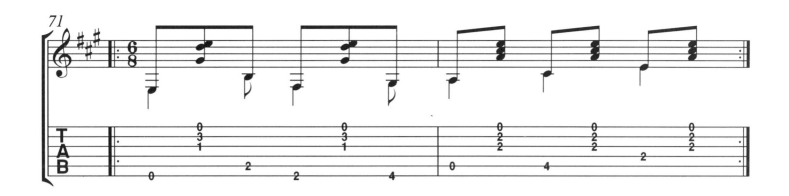

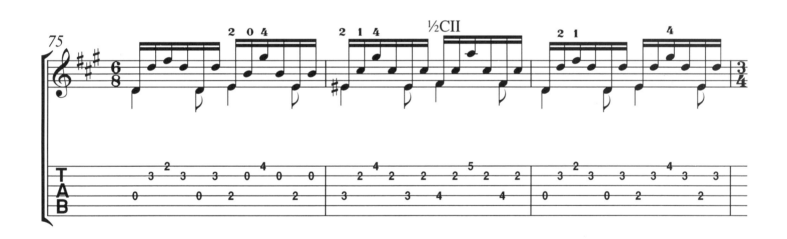

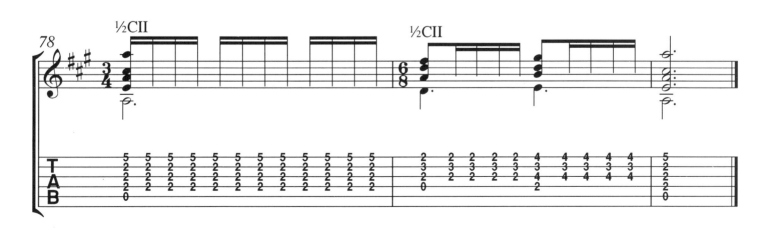

Cachita

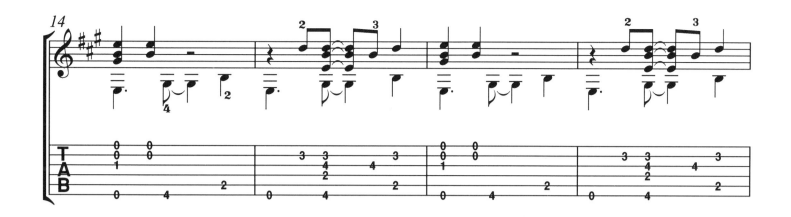

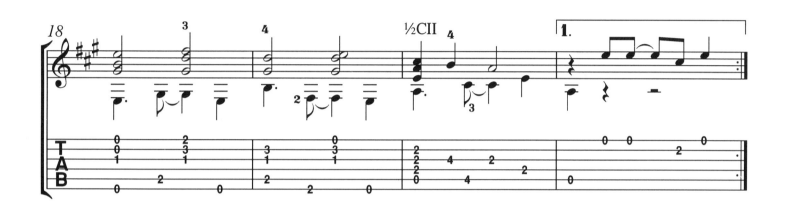

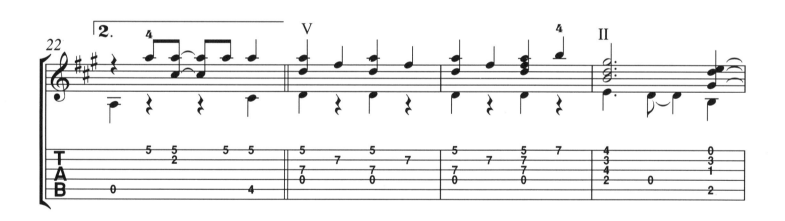

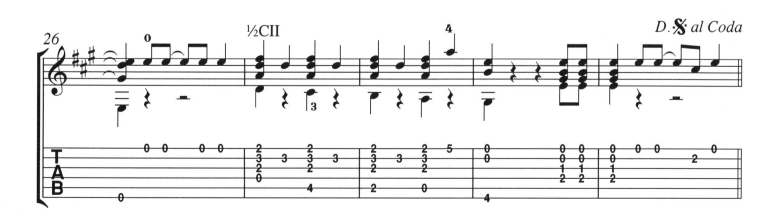

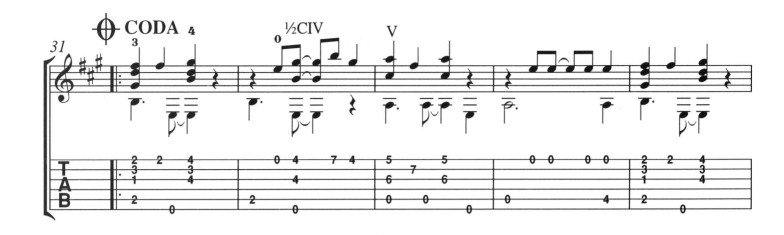

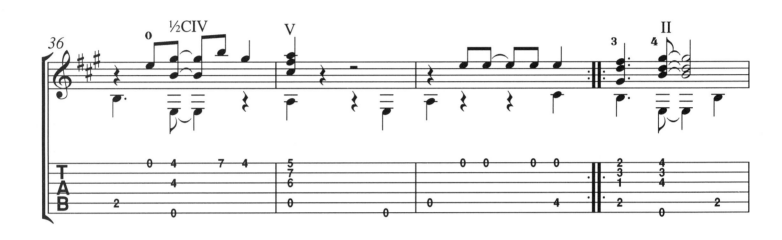

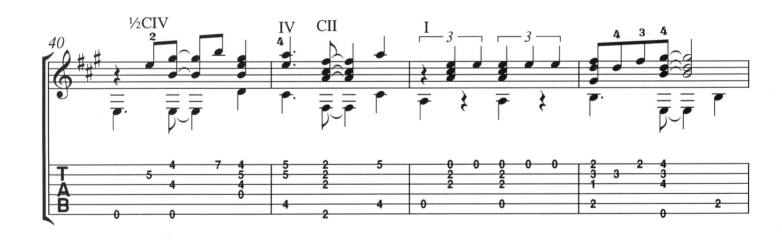

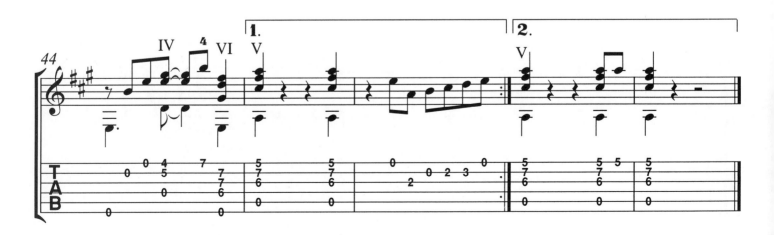

Siempre En Mi Corazón
Always In My Heart

Ernesto Lecuona
Arr. John Zaradin

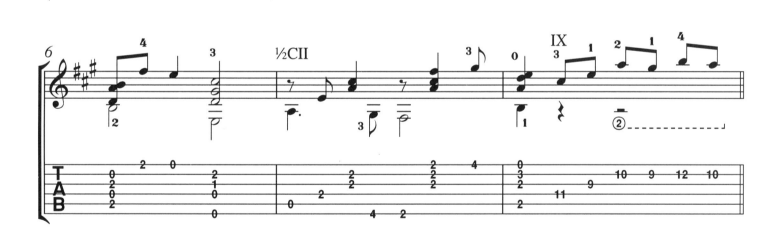

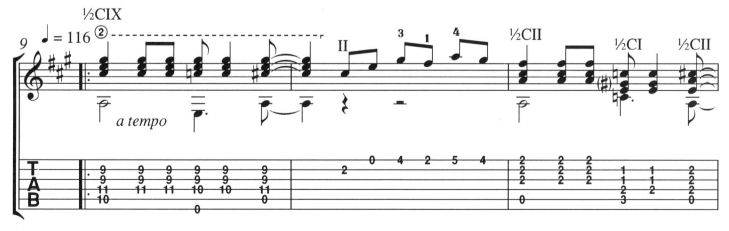

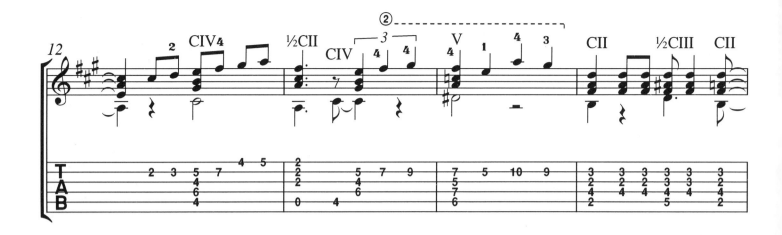

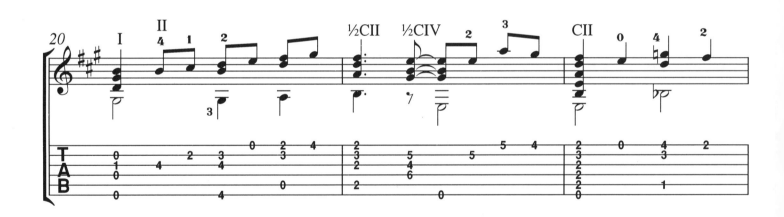

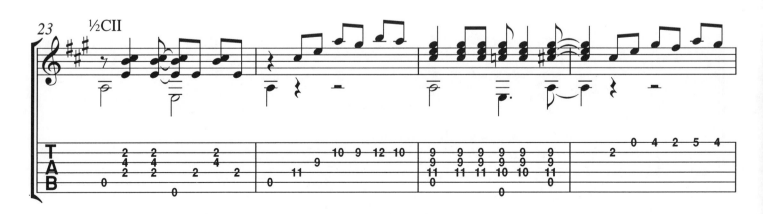

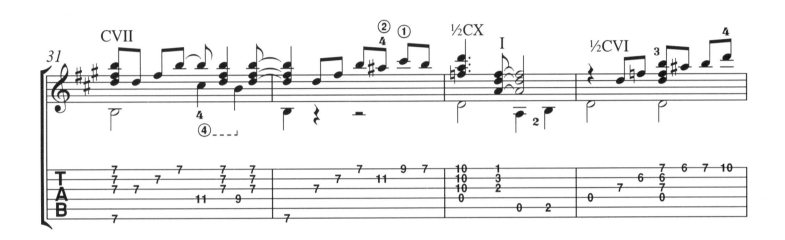

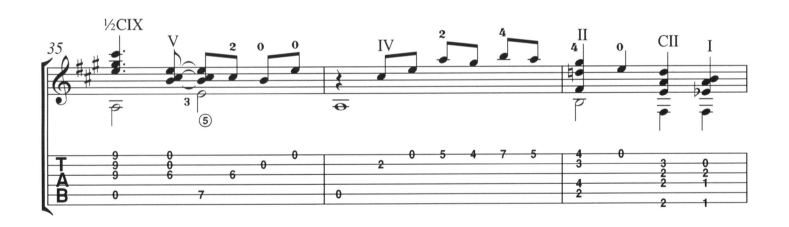

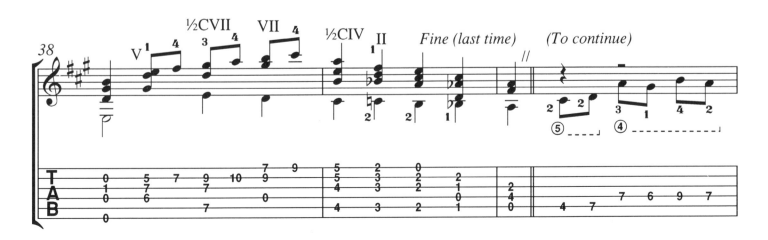

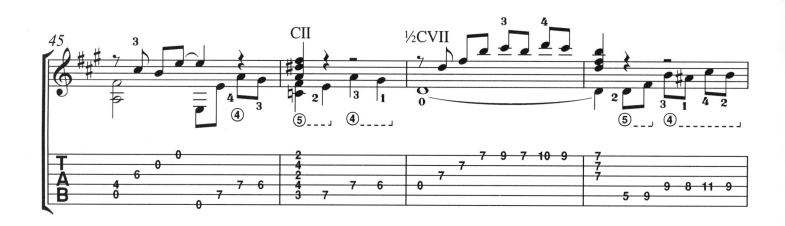

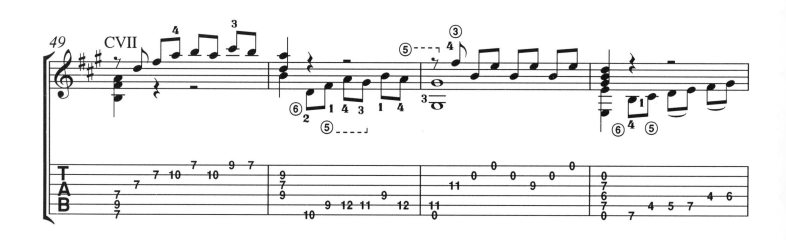

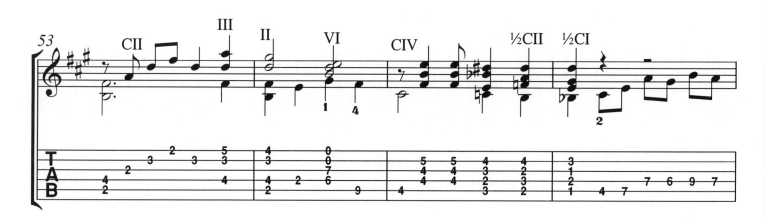

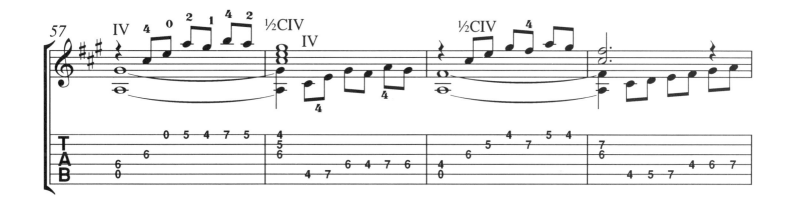

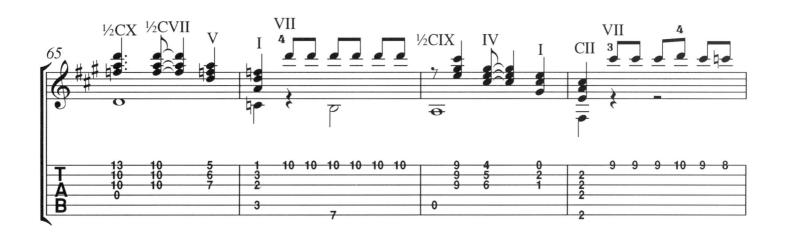

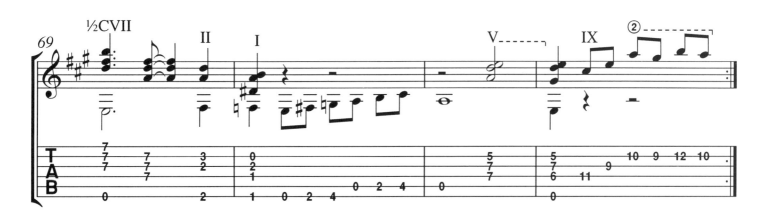